The Real... Selling Y...

Learn to Think Like a Buyer

TABLE OF CONTENTS

	Introduction to Woodbridge International	1
Chapter 1	What is the Golden Rule?	5
Chapter 2	What Is Your Future Story?	13
Chapter 3	Why Does Due Diligence Delay Closing the Deal?	23
Chapter 4	Who Is Going to Operate the Business Post-Sale? The Future Team.	35
Chapter 5	Can You Come Down Off the Throne?	47
Chapter 6	What Are the Risky Elements in Your Business?	61
Chapter 7	Is Your Business Sustainable? Beware of Self-Limiting Assumptions	69
Chapter 8	Is Your Business Defendable?	81
Chapter 9	Selecting Your Deal Attorney	91
Chapter 10	Summing Up: The Buyer's Perspective	99

Introduction to Woodbridge International

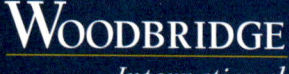

WOODBRIDGE
International
Mergers & Acquisitions Since 1993

Robert Koenig
Founder and CEO

We love entrepreneurs and business owners.
You move the economy.
You move our civilization forward.

You spend a substantial amount of your life building a business, and then – when you are ready to move on, cash in your chips – it's challenging to monetize the business; to find a buyer who offers you a fair market value and deal structure.

For almost 30 years, Woodbridge has been dedicated to positively transforming the lives of business owners by selling their businesses. We are proud of our contribution to leveling the playing field for business owners – by establishing a market for their business.

A recent client was approached by a buyer, offering a $19 million letter of intent (LOI). The client turned down this offer and selected Woodbridge, saying: "I sensed I was uneducated. I'm in over my head. It's better to get an expert team on my side."

Specialized insight and support for selling your business are even more important with the recent parade of black swan events. Whether it's the pandemic, supply line disruptions or shortages of key employees, you benefit from selecting an advisor geared to selling a business in disruptive times.

This is our 7th book in a series to provide you, the business owner, with insights for selling your business. This book focuses on the buyer's mindset.

All too often, business owners get locked into the seller's mindset, and insufficiently consider the buyer's mindset. This causes many deals to fail, or to generate lower offers.

For instance, you may have a fully depreciated machine which works just fine – no problem from the seller's perspective. The buyer may look at the same fully depreciated machine and think, "I need to set aside $500,000 to replace that machine." This affects how the buyer values your business. Considering the buyer's perspective helps you develop a fair and reasonable valuation for your business and attracts more buyers.

Each chapter begins with a question from the buyer's perspective. We want to arm you to answer these questions.

Are you ready?
Prepare yourself for an exciting journey into the buyer's mindset.

Characters in this Book

Bob Co-founder of the "Seller's Club – recently sold his business through an auction process; initially tried to sell it himself

Jill Co-founder of the "Seller's Club – recently sold her business through an auction process; introduced Bob to her M&A firm

Jim Successful business owner trying to sell his business by himself

Sam Partner in private equity group; finds target companies to acquire by outreach, calling business owners

Alan Partner at an M&A firm

WOODBRIDGE
International

1764 Litchfield Turnpike | Suite 250 | New Haven, CT 06525
203.389.8400 | woodbridgegrp.com

Chapter 1
What Is The Golden Rule?

> How do I get a fair price for my business?
> *The First-Time Seller's Question*
>
> The golden rule: Whoever has the gold rules.
> *The Buyer's Handbook*
>
> An auction provides options and leverage.
> *The Seller's Handbook*

WOODBRIDGE
International
Mergers & Acquisitions Since 1993

Jim's mind was racing as he walked to his 9 a.m. meeting. He had done the impossible – found a legitimate buyer for his business!

It took him 18 years to build his business into a well-oiled machine – $10 million in sales, $2 million in EBITDA. When he signs the LOI later today, he will be well on his way to an $8.5 million payday, 60% cash at closing, with a seller's note for the balance, to be paid out over three years – after the buyer completes due diligence.

At the thought of due diligence, he groaned. He had heard some war stories, especially from his CPA. Then, he smiled again.

Everyone had told him it was the wrong way to go – "get some expert help," they said! Absurd. Jim knew better.

He had always done things himself and when he signs the LOI today, he will have the proof without wasting money on M&A fees.

But his CPA was such a nudge – "speak to the Seller's Club," he insisted. "Fine, I will do it."

Attend the Seller's Club meeting at 9 a.m., then sign the LOI at noon – he could taste his future. Directly ahead was the coffee shop; he liked the subtle smell of coffee.

Inside, Bob and Jill were having their weekly cup of Joe. They had recently sold their respective businesses, and continued their weekly meetings, now in the 5th year. They were young enough to look for a business in which they could both invest, expanding their friendship into a business partnership.

Bob and Jill had used the same M&A firm to sell their businesses. The M&A firm specialized in an auction, developing and marketing the one-page blind teaser describing their business to as many as 10,000 potential buyers. The marketing generated 17 bids for Jill's business and 23 bids for Bob's business.

Jill's accountant had asked them to talk to Jim; the CPA thought Jim was acting rashly, leaving money on the table, by selling the business himself.

Jim opened the coffee shop door, scanned the room, recognized Bob and Jill from their LinkedIn profiles and quickly walked over to them.

Standing, Jim said: "Look, today's a big day for me, lots to do. I sign the LOI to sell my business at noon. My CPA insisted I talk to you guys, fine, I'm here. What do you have to say?"

Bob said: "Why not sit down, join us. Have a cup of coffee."

Jim: "No time for that, just give me the straight skinny. Any reason I shouldn't sign the LOI today?"

Bob's first reaction was to let Jim waltz off into LOI hell. Death of a thousand cuts in due diligence. Didn't seem to be worth the trouble.

Jill was a little more sympathetic and said:

"When is your closing date?"

Jim fired back: "As soon as possible, of course – time is of the essence. As you know, time kills all deals."

Bob said: "I tried to sell my business myself. I signed an LOI with a similar clause, 'as soon as possible.' After nine months of bleeding in due diligence, with one delay after another, Jill here convinced me to meet with her M&A firm, who did a proper auction. They never accept an LOI without a firm closing date. Sold my business in five months – 60 days in due diligence."

Jim was startled. He walked over to the counter, ordered coffee and sat down. He wanted to hear more.

Across town, Sam, the managing partner of a private equity (PE) firm, was preparing to meet Jim at noon, to sign the LOI.

Sam was excited as he contemplated the day ahead, and his application of the golden rule: "Whoever has the gold rules!" Sam's PE firm had an uncanny knack of finding sellers who needed their gold, and had few options, making the seller more committed emotionally and financially to the deal. In fact, they had four full-time team members calling business owners in their sweet spot, looking for owners without M&A representation. That's how he had found Jim.

Sam liked Jim, liked his business. Jim was very independent, took responsibility for his fate and always did everything himself. Consequently, Jim was selling the business by himself, focused on saving the M&A fees.

They both had smiled when Jim said: "I'm not wasting fees on an M&A firm, when I can clearly get it done myself."

Sam grinned, thinking about the noon meeting. With Jim, Sam's private equity firm was the market. He had the gold and would set the rules, reeling Jim in, a little at a time. Probably extending the closing date, through sequential due diligence requests, to monitor Jim's results. He relished the day ahead.

This Really Happened – Case Histories

For most owners, without a well-established market for the business, the selling owner must rely on the buyer's claims. You have no leverage.

The one buyer the owner finds becomes the actual market; this undermines your business sale, because without competition, there is no sense of buyer urgency. Sellers suffer in two ways:

- Less money is offered for the business
- Unfavorable payment terms, with less cash at closing

For instance, Woodbridge had been talking to a distributor for over a year. The owner had initially been excited to find a well-funded strategic buyer by himself. And thus, was tolerant, relative to the due diligence delays. The buyer was offering $12 million, 6x EBITDA, with $8 million cash at close, the rest in a seller's note. The owner's lawyer strongly encouraged the seller to take the deal, if only they could close it. The deal kept on lagging; the buyer was stretching out due diligence.

The seller had two concerns:

- Was this a fair deal?
- Why was this taking so long?

The delays and future payout ultimately dispirited the seller enough to consider an alternative – the Woodbridge Way.

We took this distributor to market – preparing strong marketing materials, including a one-page teaser, a confidential information memo and a two-minute marketing video. We received 27 bids for the business, including a new offer from the initial strategic buyer. Prior to the auction, the strategic buyer wouldn't offer more money. Now, in the midst of competition and fear of losing the deal the strategic buyer raised the offer to $13 million cash at closing. However, we selected a different buyer with a better offer and closed this deal for $16 million, all cash at closing. Note: The seller was not only pleasantly surprised at the deal outcome, he was also surprised he didn't know the buyer.

How is it possible a "well-funded strategic buyer" only offered $12 million, with only $8 million at closing and Woodbridge's process could do so much better – one-third higher selling price with double the cash at closing?

There are at least three factors at play here:

- Competition will drive price, terms, value, and structure.

- Different buyers value the same enterprise differently, taking into account many decision-making factors including strategic appetite, perceived risk and the future story. This is one reason you need to canvass the entire market – to find the buyers who most highly value your business.

- Business buyers – like any buyer – make money by buying cheap and selling higher – not the other way. When a buyer knows they are the "only game in town" it encourages a lower price.

This story illustrates what a buyer loves: Identifying a great business like yours without a clear market value – a blind item, in effect. (In fact, many firms have a sales team calling business owners, seeking those with no M&A representation; these sellers would be at a huge disadvantage when negotiating.)

Then, buying the business at a discounted price because the owner hasn't canvassed the market. And here's the kicker: The owner is grateful for the same reason – happy to have sold the business, and never had a sense as to it's worth.

You don't want to be in this picture, do you?

Key Takeaways:

- *Entrepreneurial, do-it-yourself, zeal can work against you when selling your business. Many owners "shoot themselves in the foot."*

- *You need expert help.*

- *Very often, one buyer is no buyer.*

- *You need competition, leverage, and options when you sell your business.*

WOODBRIDGE International

1764 Litchfield Turnpike | Suite 250 | New Haven, CT 06525
203.389.8400 | woodbridgegrp.com

Chapter 2
What is Your Future Story?

> I have great financial statements. Why does this 'future story stuff' matter?
> > **The First-Time Seller's Question**
>
> We are buying the company's future. Ideally, the business has a great future, but the seller doesn't demonstrate this. So, we buy a great future, without paying for it.
> > **The Buyer's Handbook**
>
> Acting on the 'burden of proof' criteria increases the value of my business to a buyer.
> > **The Seller's Handbook**

WOODBRIDGE
International
Mergers & Acquisitions Since 1993

Jim wanted to hear more about the importance of having a closing date in the letter of intent (LOI). He asked:

"What difference does it make? If the buyer needs more time, what are you going to do?"

Jill asked: "Do you have any options, any alternative buyers?"

Jim: "No, I considered myself lucky to have the one buyer."

Jill: "Have you ever heard the saying, 'One buyer is no buyer?' Before we focus on the closing date, we should discuss the importance of options. To have options – many potential buyers – it's important to have a strong future story. This creates FOMO – fear of missing out."

Jim could see this might take some time. Maybe he could stay for 20-30 minutes, and still make his noon LOI signing.

He sighed and said:

"Tell me about the future story."

Jill shared this background:

"At the core, your buyer is interested in and purchasing the future of your business – seeking a 3x-10x return on investment. Typically, this requires substantially growing your business, probably at least doubling profitability in the next 3-5 years. The buyer will want to know: How will I do this?

Many sellers think their 'future story work' is done when they submit financials – whether audited or not audited – for the last 3-5 years. These sellers think 'let the buyer tell me what the business is worth.' Thought question: Will this approach get you the best deal for your business?

Jim objected: "Wait a moment, slow down. I don't have a crystal ball. I can't predict the future. And I don't want to be responsible for saying sales will double. What if they don't? Will I have to give back my payout?"

Bob thought it was time to discuss the burden of proof criterion:

"The burden of proof is on the person who says something is so. You are right in thinking if you project a strong future story – strong profitable sales growth in the future – the buyer is going to want to know why this is believable.

This is probably the hardest part of preparing to sell your business."

Jim was curious: "This makes sense, what is involved in a future story."

Bob said: "Your financials do not map out the future. They are no substitute for telling the business future story – how it might grow, what new products or services you might offer. No one knows your business and its possibilities as you do.

Your buyer isn't going to pay you for the possibilities they develop."

Jim asked: "Are you saying I can't sell my business without a strong future story?"

Jill commented: "Not at all; you already have an LOI for your business. The question is not, Can you sell the business? The question is, Are you getting the right price and deal structure? Meaning the most cash you can get at closing."

Jim wanted to know: "Does the future story mostly help with negotiating the best LOI?"

Jill observed: "Actually it drives the whole selling process. Your future story isn't something to introduce as you negotiate your best deal with a buyer.

The future story is used during the entire marketing process, to achieve the most robust auction – the most bidders with certainty to close, offering the most money and best deal structure, especially cash at closing.

When you develop your powerful one-page blind teaser to attract the right buyers' attention as you go to market, your future story will pull them in and create FOMO – fear of missing out."

"Can you be more specific," asked Jim, "about what goes into a future story?"

Bob responded:

"You will want to show the buyer how the business can increase sales with new:

- Products/services
- Market segments
- Marketing
- Sales team members
- New locations

Other positive future story factors can include backlogs, long-term contracts, acquisitions and especially your management team.

Buyers also love to hear about your B-list of opportunities."

Jim asked: "What's the B-list?"

Bob said: "All of those great ideas you had, started to develop, but never brought to fruition. It shows the buyer great expansion opportunities."

Jim wanted to know: "How do I prove there's value when I haven't implemented a plan?"

Jill said: "If there are no actual sales for a new concept – documentation of interest can still be helpful. For instance, if you have correspondence stating a prospect or customer wants to:

- Franchise or license your concept
- Bring your product or service to a new geography
- Substantially increase purchases of existing items bought

Jim was quiet for a minute. This was a lot to take in, only two hours before signing an LOI. Suddenly, his eyes narrowed, and he said:

"Wait a second, how could you possibly know I don't already have the best deal right now? Haven't you ever heard the saying, 'your first offer is your best offer'?"

Jill responded: "Of course we don't know this for sure. It's the rule of reason. Think about the process. Doesn't it make sense you will get bigger and better LOIs if:

- You show a powerful future story
- The buyers realize they are in competition, and as a result
- You have 15 bids andbring 3-5 strong contenders to a management meeting"

Jim was thoughtful again, reviewing the entire discussion, wondering if he had taken the best approach to selling his business. He looked at his watch. Maybe he could stay another 30-60 minutes and still have plenty of time for the LOI signing – if he decided to go through with it!

Sam, of course, knew nothing about Jim's conversation at the Seller's Club. However, Jim – and the LOI signing – were definitely on his mind.

Sam thought about the future story he would build with Jim's business, particularly building on the B-list of opportunities.

Fortunately, Jim didn't realize what a goldmine his future story could deliver – and so Sam wouldn't have to pay for it. This was often the case, when his marketing team identified a seller without a M&A advisor, who usually identified this value.

Sam had teased out the future story at one meeting, in a few questions about the possibilities. For instance, when he asked: "If I gave you a blank check, how would you invest it?"

This had led to the "B-List" discussion – all the possible new products and services on the drawing board, which Jim hadn't brought to market. Sam was thrilled to hear about all the protypes and proofs of concept, which for some reason never made it to full roll-out.

Sam was anxious to begin exploiting these possibilities, after confirming his positive impressions with a thorough due diligence, which might be done in 60 days or maybe might take more than 60 days…

This Really Happened – Case Histories

After you go to market and send out your one-page teaser, prospective buyers who show interest will sign an NDA – a nondisclosure agreement. In return, they will receive your CIM – the confidential information memorandum – which provides enough information for buyers to submit a non-binding bid. Once you receive all your bids – **we typically get about 20 bids at Woodbridge** – you decide who you want to meet in a management meeting.

The management meeting is your chance to "sell" your company. Your potential buyers will be very interested in hearing more about your future story. It's what brought them to the dance.

Here's where the B-list of ideas you never implemented can be very powerful.

You may have already developed some great business ideas – but, unless you quantify them and show evidence for them, the buyer will probably not pay you for these ideas.

As one management meeting was ending, the buyer asked about a potential innovation for the company. The seller talked about the idea being on their "B list" of non-implemented business concepts. The buyer became animated and instead of ending the meeting, launched a high energy 45-minute exploration of the B-list. Be sure to bring this list to your management meetings! It catalyzes the future story discussion.

Woodbridge recently sold an air purifier company with $2.5 million of EBITDA for $15 million cash at closing with another $5 million in potential earnout. The buyer – one of six strong bidders – was a large publicly traded company. The key to this competitive auction was the future story.

Is there always a future story? When the business sells, the buyer sees a future story. The question is, Will you be properly compensated for the future story? For the most robust auction, the most qualified bidders – those with certainty to close – you want to present a strong future story.

Two years ago, Woodbridge sold a Canadian company which produced and sold one product to one customer – 100% concentration, a very risky proposition for most buyers. The company was the world's lowest-cost producer for its one product and had EBITDA exceeding $10 million. By doing an exhaustive auction, we found a buyer who loved the future story – taking this product to new markets in the United States, which they had already penetrated with other products. The product was a perfect fit. The future story justified a selling price of $60 million (US dollars).

The buyer will research your business thoroughly and make plans for how to grow sales. You won't get credit for their future efforts in the selling price.

Here's an example of an ineffective presentation of the future story:

"We are in a highly fragmented market. No company has more than 3% of the total market. You can easily double sales by acquiring my competition."

This may be true. But the seller did nothing to help achieve doubling sales. They might get some credit in the selling price if instead the narrative was:

"We are in a highly fragmented market. No company has more than 3% of the total market. You can easily double sales by acquiring my competition. I am currently talking to three competitors about acquiring them and have a signed LOI for one of them."

One moral of these stories – don't prejudge who your buyer will be. There are lots of buyers out there if you know where to look – and we know where to look!

From selling hundreds of companies, we realize owners can have challenges with this most-important part of the process.

One of our favorite sayings is: "Be a success, not a failure statistic." We will finish this chapter with a story which almost ended in disaster over the future story.

We had a challenge selling one great, well-established company, with about $2.5 MM of EBITDA, where the owner didn't want to project a future story. Believe it or not, in the management meetings, the owner tried to talk the buyer out of buying the business! The buyer would say, "could we sell your product to these new customers?" And the owner would respond – "that's a bad idea, to acquire new customers. You would have credit risk."

You may not be surprised to hear we sold that business despite the owner, not because of the owner. The key was ultimately convincing the owner to focus on the future story, in a positive way – and coaching the owner in how to tell the future story.

We developed a special training program for owners to think like a buyer, in large part because of experiences like this. Too many owners don't know what is required to optimally sell their business, to find out what their business is worth, because they can't enter the buyer's mindset.

A strong future story is key to successfully selling your business.

Key Takeaways:

- Buyers are seeking a 3x-10x return on their investment.

- They get this return through implementing the future story of your business – they are buying the future story.

- Properly developed, your future story creates FOMO – fear of missing out.

- You and your M&A resource uses FOMO to control the process.

- Be guided by the burden-of-proof principle – the burden of proof is on the person who asserts something is so.

WOODBRIDGE
International

1764 Litchfield Turnpike | Suite 250 | New Haven, CT 06525
203.389.8400 | woodbridgegrp.com

Chapter 3
Why Does Due Diligence Delay Closing the Deal?

" I have a good deal, why is it taking so long to finish due diligence and close the sale?
>> **The First-Time Seller's Question**

The seller can wait.
>> **The Buyer's Handbook**

Time kills all deals.
>> **The Seller's Handbook** "

Jim glanced at his watch – 10 a.m. He wasn't quite ready to postpone his noon meeting with Sam, but Jim was getting a little anxious. He had a better sense of the future story, and now wanted to ask more questions about due diligence. Jim steered the conversation, saying:

"I think we took a detour, discussing the future story. You were about to tell me why a firm closing date in the LOI – as opposed to ASAP – is so important."

Jill said: "Experience shows buyers can significantly delay the closing date through an extended due diligence, if the buyer isn't held to a drop-dead closing date."

Jim asked: "Why would a buyer do this?"

Jill pointed out: "There isn't one simple answer which covers all cases.

Sometimes, it's just because buyers are very busy and apply the golden rule – it's easiest to push you off than, for example, skip a board meeting.

Usually, however, it's more strategic than that. The buyer wants some insurance your business will continue performing post-closing. By extending the due diligence period, they closely monitor your business performance over a longer period.

If EBITDA drops, they can seek a re-trade – a lower price. If EBITDA holds steady, this reassures the buyer; it's a risk mitigation strategy. When there are no options, most sellers go along with these delays. If EBITDA grows the buyer isn't likely to raise their bid.

We discussed how the future story develops options and keeps the buyer honest – in case the buyer wants to delay closing the sale."

Many times, sellers shoot themselves in the foot. They aren't prepared for due diligence, they haven't researched the needed documents and put them in the virtual data room. Under intense emotional pressure of managing the business while in due diligence, they now must hunt down the documents and pull them all together. This causes delays the buyer can reasonably blame on the seller. The transaction is stalled – which the buyer wants – but the seller gets the blame.

Jim was becoming more and more uncomfortable with signing the LOI at his noon meeting, realizing he lacked strategic context and advice. His initial decision to save the M&A fees wasn't looking as clever as it did 60 minutes ago.

Jim asked: "Why do sellers allow this to happen?"

Bob remembered his own experience and shared these thoughts:

"More commonly, it's because we – as first-time sellers – don't know the market. The buyer takes advantage of our lack of experience, saying something like:

'I've been doing deals for 30 years; this is how it's done. We are going to complete due diligence just as soon as we can.'

What does this mean? 60 days? 90 days? A year?

The buyer has taken control of the timeline – and time doesn't favor the seller. It kills all deals.

If you don't have an experienced advisor strongly advocating for you, how can you refute this position?"

Jim realized this made sense and said: "I see your point. Having representation can make a difference."

Bob continued: "Just having representation isn't enough; you need the right representation.

Buyers not only push around owners selling the business by themselves. This usually happens if the seller retains a weak M&A advisor.

I had a friend who used an M&A firm specializing in my friend's industry. She took the CIM to competitors, and secured only one bid, one LOI. And, as you know, one offer is no offer. They had a target close date in the LOI.

However, buyers are accustomed to weak M&A firms who don't require buyers to stick to the timeline. These M&A firms may lead you into an LOI ill prepared for due diligence. (In large part, because these M&A firms don't generate enough options for you. That's why we discussed the future story first.)

Whether you sell by yourself or select a weak M&A firm, this typically allows buyers to push the seller around, making you conform to the buyer's terms – regardless of what was signed in an LOI."

Jim was beginning to see the possibility of his beautiful future collapsing in front of him.

Jill added to the conversation:

"Time passes, which doesn't favor the seller. On the one hand, a negative development can occur, depressing EBITDA; on the other hand the buyer is often psychologically wearing down the seller.

The buyer is saying: 'I love your business; I just need a little more time.'

It turns into death by a thousand cuts. First, it's a two-week delay, then another two weeks, which leads to a month, two months… six months…nine months. The seller becomes exhausted and frequently is prey to a re-trade, lowering the offer, just to 'get the deal done.'

When you have options, you can honestly and strongly say to the stalling buyer: 'We're going back to market or we're going to select another buyer. The company's value is not dependent on one buyer.'"

Jim valued this education. He wanted more detail; including a heads up about specific tactics buyers use to delay the transaction.

Jill said: "Here are major causes of delay in due diligence:

- No closing date in the Letter of Intent (LOI).
- Seller goes into due diligence ill prepared, without assembling materials needed prior to signing an LOI and deal momentum suffers.
- Buyer does not have the capital needed to close, and has to raise the money – this is called an "independent sponsor". A sure ticket to slowing down a deal.

Here's how they operate: first they find a deal they like – your company – then they look for the funding.

The problem for sellers: Questionable certainty to close makes them a risky buyer. Sellers often wind up fruitlessly giving extension after extension to independent sponsors who are 'raising capital.'

In general, sellers always preferred funded strategic buyers, to drive certainty to close."

Jim said: "We don't have this problem; the buyer is a funded private equity group."

Jill continued: "That can be encouraging. Here are additional stalling tactics used:

- Buyers and/or their advisers are 'overworked' – they need time to get the deal done, lacking bandwidth.
- Never-ending questions, asked sequentially over time; with an unprepared seller, this can extend due diligence 3-9 months.
- Running due diligence in sequence, not parallel – first we will do a quality of earnings check, then insurance, then HR, then legal, then the Purchase and Sales document, etc. This adds months to the due diligence process.
- Taking time to draft the LOI.
- The seller's financials are in disarray, need reworking and restating according to GAAP.
- The company's financial performance starts declining; the buyer will express interest and patience, needing to wait until performance improves consistent with projections.
- The buyer's lawyer wants to run up the bill.

This last point is why you should check your potential buyer's lawyer before signing an LOI, to see if the lawyer will delay the deal and run up your legal costs. You need strong advisors – an M&A firm, an experienced M&A lawyer for your business and a lawyer for yourself – to make sure the buyer is being fair and reasonable, to know what is market."

Jim said: "Quite a curriculum for delaying transactions. Among so many other things, I never considered checking out the buyer's lawyer. Forewarned is forearmed. I am very grateful to you. Sounds like I need better advice and advisors, to guide me as to what is fair and reasonable."

Bob wanted to know: "What are you going to do at your noon meeting with the private equity firm."

Jim said: "Ask questions. Thanks for all your help. I think I would like to stop by and visit you next week."

Bob said: "You are welcome, any time."

Jim had a lot on his mind, as he walked to the LOI signing meeting. It was a brisk, cold day, which helped him clear his mind. He decided to focus on the closing date in the meeting.

His lawyer had vetted and OK'd the LOI; but, in retrospect, Jim wondered if his lawyer had enough knowledge to properly advise him. True, the lawyer had helped with contracts and labor matters for 20 years. But it began to seem like selling your business was unique, different than like selling products and services on a day-to-day basis. Did he have the right lawyer?

Refocusing on the meeting, Jim decided to test the buyer by addressing the closing date.

Sam glanced at the clock in the conference room; Jim would be there within a few minutes. He had Jim's favorite beverage and sandwich ready for a friendly working lunch, which would end with signing the LOI.

And then…building Jim's business, getting a 10x return on the investment could begin. Sam thought about his report to the shareholders in 2-3 years. It would begin:

"The purchase, development, and sale of Jim's business is a great example of the power of our system. Our business developers find 'diamonds in the rough', great businesses without representation. We are able to buy the businesses on very favorable terms, then develop and sell them at a great profit."

His reverie was interrupted by a knock on the door; Jim had arrived.

The meeting started on a friendly tone. Jim was famished from his morning meeting and enjoyed the meal. They chatted about family and vacations.

Having warmed Jim up, Sam casually asked: "Are there any questions you have about the LOI, before we OK it?"

Jim asked: "Just one for now. As I read it over this morning, I realized it didn't have a closing date in it. Why is that?"

Sam was surprised this question arose at the 11th hour and 59th minute. Warning bells sounded in his head. He replied:

"As you know, once we sign the LOI, my firm will begin due diligence. There are so many imponderables – so much beyond both of our firms' control – that we acknowledge 'time is of the essence' and we complete due diligence ASAP."

Jim said: "I was talking to a colleague today, who recently sold his business. Due diligence dragged on for nine months. He said his major learning was: have a binding closing date in the LOI. Any reason why we can't have a 60-day due diligence period?"

Sam thought to himself: 'Aha, now I understand the question about closing date. I may just have a challenge.' He squirmed in his seat a bit. It was company policy to have the option to extend due diligence – when deemed appropriate – to monitor the seller's business. Of course, he couldn't say this. He decided to test how important this was to the seller; did he really want to sign the LOI today. Could he tolerate a delay? Sam said out loud:

"I will have to take this back to the investment committee for approval of a firm closing date. I know what they will ask – 'is the seller afraid something bad will happen? What difference does it make if due diligence takes 60 days or 120 days?'"

Jim smiled. He was OK with the delay, as he was leaning toward changing how he sold his business. Sam's response convinced him to continue doing research on other options. Maybe, just maybe, paying an M&A fee would be the **least expensive** way to sell his business.

This Really Happened – Case Histories

The seller had a strong manufacturing business and found a strategic buyer by herself, with a great deal value – 6.5x EBITDA. The buyer kept on stretching out the closing date, ultimately taking nine months.

Why did this happen? The seller was not prepared for a conventional due diligence. She didn't have an advisor who coached her on preparing the virtual data room before she was in market. She became prey to a "stalling" buyer who made sequential requests for information which the seller should have had in the virtual data room from the outset. Again, this can add 6-12 months to the process.

Finally, the seller was sufficiently aggravated by the delays, and came to Woodbridge. We quickly went to market, securing 30 bids and closed a deal for 7.5x EBITDA in five months. A large private equity firm made the purchase to strategically enhance one of its portfolio companies.

Woodbridge minimize delays in due diligence by:

- Helping our clients prepare, having most of the information needed for due diligence in the virtual data room – before management meetings
- Using FOMO to insist on rigorous adherence to the 150-day timeline
- Generating options with an auction – so that we can go back to market if a buyer isn't taking us seriously.

We will always try to get the deal done with the right buyer – a fair and reasonable deal, with certainty to close. But on some occasions, if a buyer's behavior is egregious, we go back to market.

The idea 'time kills all deals' reflects we don't know what we don't know. We don't know what black swan events – unpredictable and materially affecting the business adversely – are right around the corner.

Here's a 'time kills all deals' example with a happy ending:

The seller had facilities in the United States and Canada. The buyer, an independent sponsor, was very excited, and succeeded in raising equity ($14 million) and bank debt ($7 million). We were days from closing when the equity investor changed its policy to no longer invest in independent sponsorship deals. This left us with a $14 million gap for financing the deal. Fortunately, the bank liked the deal so much, they stepped in and financed the gap.

If we close on the closing date, later black swan events are of no consequence. Therefore, it's essential to have a firm closing date and closely monitor the buyer's progress in due diligence.

One last thought on your responsiveness to legitimate buyer information requests in due diligence – how you respond sends an important message to the buyer.

If you don't provide timely legitimate information to a buyer before you close, before money is wired to your account, what will the buyer think about your level of commitment post-closing? If the buyer needs you for some transitional period, will the buyer see you as reliable? Or will the buyer think: "Once you have your money, you're out of here." If you are seen as essential to a transition, this might even kill the deal.

How can you reduce risks that could kill your deal?

Key Takeaways:

- *Many buyers delay due diligence to monitor your performance.*

- *To protect yourself, you need to adhere to a strict timeline for closing.*

- *Your strongest tool for managing the process is a strong future story, which creates FOMO – fear of missing out.*

- *Your M&A resource knows what is market; that is, which requests by the buyer are reasonable, which are not. Be guided by your M&A resource.*

- *Being prepared for due diligence and having the virtual data room complete prior to signing the LOI will be instrumental to staying on track to the closing date.*

Chapter 4

Who Is Going to Operate the Business Post-Sale? The Future Team.

> I don't want to introduce the buyer to my employees until after the deal is done. Too risky. Why should I take this chance?
>
> — *The First-Time Seller's Question*
>
> How can I get comfortable with the future team of this business if I don't meet them?
>
> — *The Buyer's Handbook*
>
> Does the burden of proof criteria apply to the future team? Let's explore this point.
>
> — *The Seller's Handbook*

WOODBRIDGE *International*
Mergers & Acquisitions Since 1993

Jim was looking forward to Seller's Club the following week. This time, he gladly sat down, when invited.

Jill smiled and asked: "How did your noon meeting go last week? Did you sign the LOI?"

Jim wasn't so sure of himself this time. "No, I didn't sign. I asked for a closing date in the LOI; the buyer said he had to run the idea past the company's investment committee. Haven't heard from him since."

Then, he smiled. "If I thought I didn't have options, I would be sweating bullets right now. In fact, I don't have any good options, unless you two will introduce me to the M&A firm you used."

Bob said: "Would you like an introduction right now? I can probably get Alan – the business development partner – on the phone."

Jim said: "There's no time like the present."

Bob reached Alan and set an appointment for Jim to meet him later that afternoon.

In the meantime, Sam was wondering how long he should make Jim wait. Sam didn't really need to go to the investment committee for approval on the closing date. Sam wanted Jim to sweat a little, realize he didn't have any options, then come back to Sam a little humbler and more compliant. There was no rush. He was just applying the golden rule.

Ironically, Jim was also in no rush, with a new door opened in his mind. He had a 2 P.M. meeting with Alan to learn about the auction method of selling his business.

The meeting opened on a very positive note. Fortunately, having talked to Bob and Jill, he was prepared to discuss his future story. Alan was impressed.

Alan reviewed the auction model with Jim:

- Start with the 1-page teaser
- Which attracts interest from prospective buyers who signed NDAs (non-disclosure agreements)
- To receive the CIM (confidential information memo) and 2-minute marketing video
- Which generate non-binding bids.

Alan concluded: "From this group of bidders, we jointly select who to invite to management meetings. We look very carefully at the buyer's culture and their certainty to close – do they have the funding?"

Jim liked this process; this would generate options he didn't have at present with Sam. He was glad to have validated the process with Bob and Jill, two successful case studies.

The conversation was moving forward smoothly until they were deep into a discussion about the future team.

Alan commented: "For the best payout, the buyer will want to see a strong future team."

Jim was glad to hear the key executive group's importance; a group he had trained and nurtured over the years. Jim would be glad to discuss the group in the management meeting. Their meeting was flowing swimmingly, until Alan said:

"Which team members might you bring into the management meeting?"

"Huh? I wasn't planning to bring in any key execs. In fact, I wasn't planning to tell anyone until I sold the business."

Alan's smile faded. He became very sober and said: "This is probably a good time to talk about 'Pay me now or pay me later. But you will pay."

"What does that mean?" asked Jim.

Alan continued:

"There will be a series of time-based trade-offs in selling your business: do it now or do it later. In general, you will almost always be better off doing it now, when selling your business. For example….

You have already heard from Bob and Jill about the importance of populating the data room as soon as possible. It's pay me now or pay me later. The more information you upload now, earlier in the process, the easier it will be to expedite the due diligence process and stick to your deal timeline, after you have a LOI (letter of intent)."

Jim wanted to know: "What does this have to do with the future team?"

Alan said:

"A similar trade-off exists regarding showing the buyer your business's future team. You already understand the future story's importance.

The future team is part of the future story; they deliver the future story."

"Slow down a minute, Alan. If I tell one to three key executives I am selling the business and invite them to the management meeting with potential buyers, I see some problems. Maybe, just maybe:

- It will get out into the marketplace, hurting my relationships with customers and vendors
- These key executives may quit
- They will lose focus and EBITDA will suffer."

Alan responded: "This is very reasonable looking at the world from the seller's perspective. This is the 'pay me now' part of the equation.

You know your management team, their taste for risk and for change. In general, most people are suspicious of change.

Where you have strong relationships with key execs, you should be able to position the sale as offering them a brighter future. They know you aren't going to work forever; they are reasonably concerned about the future and your transition plan should stem some concerns.

They will be excited by the opportunity to be involved in the process, to meet potential buyers, and provide input to your decision. In a management meeting, key execs can discuss how they have contributed to build your business, what they are proud of – and also the potential future story they see, what they are excited by. Buyers love to see passion.

Your execs will be pleasantly surprised to learn in the management meeting just how important they are to the buyer."

Jim remembered a comment he heard at Sellers' Club – about a private equity owner who said he wouldn't issue an LOI if he didn't meet the future team.

Alan observed: "Consider the buyer's perspective. If you were buying a business, wouldn't you want to meet the future team?

In our research, we have repeatedly heard from buyers that 60%-80% of the management meeting's value is evaluating the culture, the values, and the team.

As the seller, we know we have a great team, we know there is no risk to the buyer. This is looking at the issue from the seller's perspective. Let's consider the buyer's perspective.

When you consider the burden-of-proof criteria, how can we best satisfy the buyer? By saying 'trust me?' Probably not – more likely, by showing the buyer your future team.

Does this mean we can't sell your company without showing the future team? Of course not. What we are discussing here is the robustness of the auction. We want the most buyers offering you the most money, and the best deal structure.

If you don't 'pay now', by showing the future team, you will probably 'pay later', by a less robust auction."

Jim thought back to the offer from Sam: Only receiving 60% in cash at closing, the balance in a seller's note. Maybe the deferred payout was partially due to the fact that Jim didn't show the future team.

Alan had given Jim a lot to think about.

A week went by, without any word from Sam, which suited Jim just fine. The following week, at Sellers' Club, Jim had a few more questions, starting with:

"Did you bring your key execs to management meetings?"

Both Jill and Bob had brought in key managers. This helped Jim some; still it seemed risky. He asked:

"When should you tell your leadership team about selling your business?"

Jill responded:

"The better your relationship with key exec team members, then sooner is better. You shouldn't be surprised to find team members excited at being part of the process and also excited at the prospect of future investment and business growth.

At the latest, you would tell team members about one week before management meetings, when you feel confident you would be meeting strong potential buyers."

Alan also wanted to know:

"Do key team members have to attend the entire management meeting?"

Bob fielded this question:

"Not at all. They can join for 'cameo appearances' of 10 minutes' duration, for which you will coach them. They don't need to hear about the finances of the deal."

Jim was still nervous and looking for options.

"Could you frame it differently than: We're looking to sell the company?"

Bob pointed out:

"Some business owners say they are looking for investors to join them, to help them grow the business, to carry some of the risk. Here are possible narratives:

- 'We have numerous business opportunities requiring more capital investment. I don't want to hold the business back. With the right investor support – sharing our vision and values – we can take this company to the moon.'

- For a more mature owner: 'With the great opportunities ahead of us, the timing is right to find an investor who shares our vision and values to help lead this company to the next level and provide a succession plan for me.'

- 'We need deeper pockets than mine to grow this business and secure your jobs for the future. The best thing for the business is to find an investor who shares our vision and values.'

Then, as the investor search continues, it may just 'turn out' one of the potential investors liked the business so much, they bought the business."

Jim felt his resistance melting. He scheduled another meeting with Alan, maybe to sign up the M&A firm.

This Really Happened – Case Histories

We had a client with an automated online digital product. It ran by itself, generating over $4 million of EBITDA; it just needed a small team for updates and fine tuning. The seller, a pioneer in the industry, was retiring. After our management meeting training, the seller realized there was a major gap in the future story – no strong successor.

Many sellers in this situation think – well, the buyer will supply a new, strong, competent CEO. They might. However, financial buyers – private equity firms – usually want to see a complete strong team in place.

So whereas we might have sold the business without a strong leader, here's what happened.

The owner did some recruiting before management meetings and actually found a new CEO, currently a key executive at the biggest competitor. The owner hired this new CEO and brought him to the management meetings. The buyer said it was a major reason they made the deal, paying the owner $32 million in cash at closing.

Sometimes, when they don't meet the team, buyers will protect themselves against their perceived risk through changing the deal structure.

We always prefer to see you get as close to 100% cash at closing as possible.

To protect themselves against uncertainty when they don't meet the team, the buyer may ask the seller to:

- Issue a seller's note, which the buyer will pay over a period of time, or
- Accept money in an earnout – when the company achieves future EBITDA targets, there are additional payments to the seller.

In 2021, we sold two distribution companies where the buyers didn't meet the future teams. It affected the deal structure:

- In the first case, the seller received 50% cash at close ($3.5 million), 20% in a seller's note, 30% in earnout.
- In the second case, with $2 million in EBITDA, the seller received $5 million cash at close, $5 million earnout over two years.

Our clients were satisfied with the deal they made. However, if they had trusted their key execs and brought them to management meetings, they would probably have received more money for their business and a better deal structure – more money at closing.

In another case, where the buyer met the executive team, we asked the buyer what he thought of our management meeting. He said it was one of the best meetings he ever attended because:

- He knows which team member will do what post-transaction, and who will take over for the departing owners.
- He met all the future leaders and he liked them.

It's not hard to see why meeting the future team can lead to an even better deal for you. Buyers are looking for passion; meeting your key execs can convey that passion.

We have management meeting training to help prepare owners like you for meeting buyers. This point – who will the buyers meet – is always an important discussion topic.

When we ask sellers what kind of discount they would want as a buyer who didn't meet the management team, we typically hear discounts of 20%-30%.

Here's a last thought. Whether or not you bring in your future team sends an important message about your culture's transparency to the buyer.

Your buyer will prefer a more transparent culture. Wouldn't you?

Key Takeaways:

- 60%-80% of the management meeting is assessing the company culture, the values, and the team.

- The future team is an essential part of your future story.

- The decision to bring in your executive team is an example of: 'pay me now or pay me later'.

- The buyer wants to be satisfied your future team can deliver the future story.

- Management meetings are an opportunity to re-engage your team, show them your company's exciting future and make them part of it.

WOODBRIDGE International

1764 Litchfield Turnpike | Suite 250 | New Haven, CT 06525
203.389.8400 | woodbridgegrp.com

Chapter 5
Can You Come Down Off the Throne?

> This business is my kingdom. I created it. Excuse me for saying this, but really, it's my way or the highway.
>> **The First-Time Seller's Question**
>
> I'm always worried if the seller can come down off the throne, having lived there so long. Is the seller humble? Does the culture encourage humility?
>> **The Buyer's Handbook**
>
> How do I convince the buyer that I am humble and coachable?
>> **The Seller's Handbook**

WOODBRIDGE
International
Mergers & Acquisitions Since 1993

Sam was getting a bit impatient. Two weeks had passed since the LOI signing that didn't take place. Over a closing date! So foolish, as Sam was going to run due diligence at his own pace, in any case. The golden rule.

At first, he expected Jim to call him back within a day or so. Then, he wondered if Jim was on a vacation.

Finally, after two weeks, he called Jim:

"So, Jim, what is your thinking about our LOI?'

"Hi Sam, so glad you called, I was meaning to call you. Look, I have been doing some research and thinking and decided I need to do a wider search for a potential buyer. I have signed up an M&A firm and would like to give them your contact information – to include in the buyer mix. Is this OK?"

Sam was furious. He had gone from totally controlling the situation to being one of many options. But he had so much time invested, had made so many glowing statements to his partners about Jim's business, that he glumly responded:

"Sure, keep me in the loop. When does the marketing go out?"

"In the next 3-4 weeks. I'll keep you posted."

Wow! thought Jim when he ended the call. That sure felt good, having options. But did I make the right decision? This M&A firm was asking for all kinds of information, maybe even exceeding what Sam required. In addition, I must update all the financials again. What a bother! Was it really necessary?

Jim decided to test out his experience at Sellers' Club the next day.

Jill and Bob were glad to see Jim early the next morning, as he brought his coffee to their regular table. Jill asked:

"So, what happened – anything new on the LOI and the closing date?"

Jim became animated, saying: "I guess I didn't tell you. I decided to sign up the M&A firm you recommended, to do a proper auction for my business. Let the market decide the company's value."

At the same moment, Bob and Jill exclaimed "Congratulations," followed by handshaking.

"But, you know," said Jim, "I'm wondering if I made the right decision. Sure, it was right for the two of you, but my business is special, it's different. They are asking for a ton of information to be uploaded to the virtual data room. What's the rush?"

Jill pointed out: "This is a challenging process, selling your business. You are probably at the slowest moment of the process, the eye of the hurricane. Remember the "pay me now or pay me later" theme we mentioned last time we met. This applies doubly so, to populating the virtual data room. Ask Bob about his experience."

Bob jumped right in: "I thought I knew better. Yes, the M&A firm pushed me to populate the data room from the outset, but I figured '150 days, I have plenty of time.' They tried their hardest to prepare me, to get me ready for due diligence. But I was stubborn. I was so accustomed to 'my way or the highway' for the last 25 years, I dragged out the process. I didn't pay 'now', but I sure paid 'later'."

"What happened?", asked Jim.

"I was done in by a 'black swan event' – you know, unpredictable and hugely impactful. The M&A firms fights for that 60-day due diligence and drop-dead closing date. But then, we need to do our part. We need to get the buyer the reasonable information needed for due diligence, in a timely fashion.

Well, I had the right buyer with certainty to close – and they were ready to close in 60 days, but I wasn't ready. I didn't follow the M&A firm's good advice. This led to a 30-day delay in closing, during which disaster struck."

Jim was on the edge of his seat. "What happened?," he asked.

"Remember the tariff war with China, started by President Trump? No one anticipated that – a true black swan event. Well, if I had closed on the drop-dead closing date, the second set of tariffs released would have been someone else's problem – the buyer's.

But I didn't close on the drop-dead closing date. Because I didn't follow the advice and properly, completely update the virtual data room. So, the second round of tariffs hit before we could close, and this reduced the value of my business, which resulted in a re-trade downward, I might add. I was paid 10% less money for my business, because I didn't keep the data room updated."

Jim didn't import any products, so he knew this wouldn't have affected his sale. But he realized the very nature of a black swan event is that you can't predict what will happen. Jim thought about the current supply line disruptions which did affect his business.

Jim felt he sure got his money's worth for investing in a cup of Joe.

He had other questions; in particular, Bob had raised a comment about "my way or the highway." Jim wanted to hear more about that. He remarked:

"I'm a bit of an independent cuss myself, the way you are Bob. How does this affect the selling process?"

Bob wanted to know: "Have you gone to the two-day management meeting training yet?"

"No, it's next week."

Jill added: "I don't want to steal their thunder, but I will offer you this thought: are you using the window and the mirror properly."

Jim wanted to know what this meant.

Jill continued: "It's a concept developed by Jim Collins, the author of Good to Great, and building on his concept of Level 5 leadership."

"What is that?" asked Jim.

"In Good to Great, Jim Collins introduces the idea of Level 5 leadership – a leader who is strong willed, competent, and humble at the same time.

Jim was already confused: "Wait a moment. Isn't it one or the other – either you are competent and dominant on the one hand, or humble on the other hand?"

Jill pointed out: "In an earlier book, Built to Last, Collins and Porras discuss the problem of: 'The Tyranny of the OR.' This is a false alternative. Great, long-lasting companies overcome false alternatives like:

- Business leader:
  'Should I make products which are good for society or earn a profit?'

- Salesperson:
  'Do you want me to sell or fill out the paperwork?'

- Owner selling a business:
  'Should I run the business to maximize EBITDA, or populate the virtual data room for due diligence?'

There are very few real life examples of a zero sum game – most transactions involve both parties winning.

When it comes to leadership, great leaders are both dominant AND humble.

This was new thinking to Jim, but he got the idea very quickly. It made sense, though he didn't see how it applied to selling his business.

Jill resumed with: "Collins offers a strong metaphor for verifying your Level 5 leadership – how you use the mirror and the window. A humble Level 5 leader uses:

- The **window** when there is success – looking out the window to give credit to the team

- The **mirror** – when there is a setback, asking: 'what else could I have done to prevent the setback?'

In a dysfunctional company, the leadership reverses the usage – looking in the mirror, patting themselves on the back when things go well, looking out the window at the team to decide who to fire when things go wrong.

Jim, the buyer is going to want to know:

- Are you a Level 5 leader?
- Do you have a Level 5 top executive team?

We already discussed the future team. I think you bought into the idea of bringing them to management meetings?"

"Yes," said Jim.

Bob joined the discussion, reminding Jim:

"The last time we met, we discussed the 'burden of proof' criteria, which instructs us to show the future team to the buyer to prove our case. I can now add: we also bring the future team to show we have Level 5 leadership. Remember: 60%-80% of the management meeting is evaluating the culture, the values, and the team.

For the best price and deal structure, we show the buyer how you and your team are humble and coachable – that you and your team can come down off the 'throne of habit.'

Expect the buyer to challenge whoever is in the management meeting, testing your humility and flexibility; for instance: testing the 'boundary conditions' of your business model. For example, can we hit the accelerator with respect to any part of the model to ramp up sales faster?"

Jim wondered if he would "measure up" to the humility test.

The conversation with Bob and Jill was on his mind the following week, when he joined management meeting training as part of the M&A process.

WOW! Two full 8-hour days of training! Just to get ready for a 90- to 120-minute management meeting with potential buyers. In the past, he had trouble sitting for an hour at a time – Jim was surprised at how engaged he was by the process.

As the facilitator unveiled the program, Jim realized how much he had to learn. Selling your business was definitely not like selling a product or service. The facilitator was discussing the humility test:

"Here's an example of a buyer's humility test at a management meeting I attended. The seller supplies high-margin products for pharmacies, with 100% subcontracted production. This company had $20 million of EBITDA and should have sold for $100 million-plus.

First the buyer commented:

'You have a very high concentration risk, generating all of your profits from six products. Why not build out the line, to say 20 products? The new items need not be as profitable. This will de-risk the business. What do you think?'

The seller responded:

'What a terrible idea! We looked at this years ago, makes absolutely no sense!'

About 15-20 minutes later, the buyer observed:

'You subcontract all your entire line to one factory. Why not vertically integrate, buy the factory? You will pick up the profit margin and lock down your source of supply.'

'Awful idea, can't believe you are suggesting this.'

A little later, the buyer said:

"You know, you sell to independent pharmacies, there is an association for independent pharmacies. Why don't we buy the association, so we can control some of our messaging and access?'

'Where do you get these terrible ideas? Makes no sense.'"

The facilitator paused and asked: "What message was the seller sending to the buyer?"

Jim knew the answer to this one: "He is saying: I am not flexible, it's my way or the highway."

The facilitator continued: "You know the saying, Jim, no good deed goes unpunished. What is the buyer thinking, when hearing this?"

Jim said: "This seller has a terrible culture; either I'm not interested in this company, I need a big discount, or I want to minimize cash at closing."

Jim thought back to the offer from Sam. A lower multiple of EBITDA than he expected, and only 60% cash at closing. Could this be Sam's way of saying Jim had a humility problem. Jim was glad he selected this M&A firm and that he was participating in the management meeting training.

The facilitator concluded the story by saying:

"You may be smiling, thinking this is an invention. If only you were there…

Not surprisingly the buyer – with $2 billion they needed to invest – passed on the opportunity. They had encountered a seller who wouldn't come down off the throne.

How would you respond in this scenario? In a management meeting, it's likely the buyer will suggest initiatives you considered historically and rejected.

Will you tell the buyer 'it's a dumb question?'

Of course not.

So, what would you say?"

Jim decided to give someone else a chance to respond. Another seller said:

"We looked at this years ago; at the time, we had more pressing opportunities. I will be glad to research what we did, update the info, and move forward on the initiative.

Or you might say:

This initiative required a major capital investment, which would necessitate borrowing. I didn't want to sign on yet another bank loan.

Or:

Interesting idea, I would be glad to run it down for you."

The facilitator concluded by mentioning:

"You should consider, in advance, which stories will persuade the buyer that your key team members are willing and able to come down off the throne of habit."

This Really Happened – Case Histories

A buyer found this story very compelling, about a seller expanding to a new channel of distribution, by coming down off the throne:

The seller designed consumer products and had them manufactured in Asia. Sales were about $10 million with $1 million in EBITDA. The VP Sales wanted to take the line to Amazon.

The owner was a brick-and-mortar fan and didn't like the online landscape initially.

The VP Sales persisted in showing the possibilities – eventually, the owner relented, leading to a 20% boost in profitable sales in the first year.

Buyers love to hear you have developed team members to take strong positions, and that you listen to those team members.

Another business owner – of home centers – expressed the idea this way: "I have strong general managers in each location. They are constantly suggesting new lines we can offer. I see myself as the devil's advocate. I push back on new expansion ideas – since I must invest in the inventory – until the bugs are worked out. I typically approve 80% of the initiatives, making the ideas much stronger along the way." This owner had developed and could showcase a team of innovative leaders who understood how to make entrepreneurial decisions.

Of course, you can choose to tell a buyer – through words or body language – its "my way or the highway." But then, you will have a very limited auction for your business.

Of course, 'all's well that ends well', as you will see in this last story.

We had a seller, who didn't know how to come down off the throne. In fact, his behavior was a major motivation for developing our management meeting training, which we now offer to all clients. His behavior was also a motivation for this book.

The owner had built an effective product testing company to about $3 million in EBITDA. Years ago, he stepped out of day-to-day management, delegating leadership to his daughter. He saw the management meetings as a last chance to be the star of the show – a last hurrah – and spent the first 15-20 minutes of management meetings talking about his golf game. The buyers were too polite to tell him his opening remarks weren't the reason they came to the meeting.

Although he didn't really contribute to the management meetings, we sold the business despite the owner, not because of him. Fortunately, he had a daughter who was a fantastic president; the buyers loved her presentations. When they bought the business for $16 million, part of the deal was making the daughter president and giving her 9% rollover equity. The daughter saved the deal.

We end with a cautionary tale about the throne. A client had signed on a $12 million LOI in January, which required staying on for three years. (The seller preferred six months.) As due diligence progressed, the client reverted to the six-month commitment; the buyer reduced the LOI to $10 million, as the future team was weak. Then came the quality of earnings report, showing overstated income. In April, the buyer offered $7 million at closing; the client could leave the business at once.

The seller, infuriated with the new, lower offer, walked away. We found a new buyer at $10 million; the buyer walked away after peeling back the onion in due diligence. In April, the original buyer made a last offer of $5 million cash at close. The seller refused to consider this. By July, the client was willing to take $1-2 million, but there were no offers. A sad finale – in August, they set up a GoFundMe site, which has received no money.

Can you come down off the throne so you won't lose the best deal?

Key Takeaways:

- *Buyers want Level 5 leaders – dominant and humble at the same time.*

- *Be prepared to show buyers you know how to use the window – giving credit to the team; and the mirror – asking yourself what you could have done when there is a setback.*

- *Be prepared for buyers to challenge your thinking and your current business model.*

- *In particular, be prepared to discuss ideas you considered and rejected.*

- *Be guided by the "burden of proof" principle – we need to show evidence that what we say is true is true.*

WOODBRIDGE
International

1764 Litchfield Turnpike | Suite 250 | New Haven, CT 06525
203.389.8400 | woodbridgegrp.com

Chapter 6

What Are the Risky Elements in Your Business?

> My business isn't risky. I have run it successfully for decades. What's all this talk about risk?
> **The First-Time Seller's Question**
>
> Will all the customers leave this business when the seller retires? What other risks do I face?
> **The Buyer's Handbook**
>
> The buyer has legitimate risk concerns. To get the best price we need to address these concerns.
> **The Seller's Handbook**

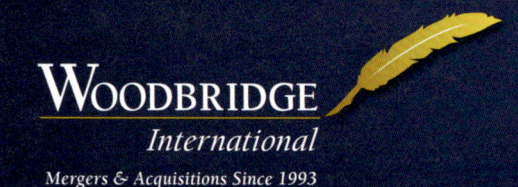

WOODBRIDGE
International
Mergers & Acquisitions Since 1993

Three months of Friday morning Sellers' Club meetings had passed. Jill and Bob were beginning to wonder if they would ever see Jim again. Maybe he decided not to sell his business.

They were evaluating a potential joint investment when who should walk in – it was Jim! They both exclaimed:

"Long time, no see."

Jim was excited:

"I made a major hire, to help sell this business!"

This sounded like the beginning of a compelling story.

Jill wanted to know: "What made you do this?"

Jim responded: "Dealing with risk aversion. You know, when we first heard about risk aversion in management meeting training, I thought 'right, maybe for other people, but this wasn't an issue for me.' Well, was it ever!"

They all thought back to their training in risk aversion and smiled. They remembered how the facilitator explained the point to the skeptical sellers…

"Risk aversion means we tend to select the less risky choice. It doesn't mean we avoid all risk, just that we try to manage it.

Daniel Kahneman helps us understand risk aversion with a classic thought experiment in his book: Thinking Fast and Slow.

This experiment will help us enter the buyer's perspective and think of how to respond to it.

Here's the "coin toss" experiment; what would you rather have:

- $5 million sure thing, wired to your account, or
- A Coin Toss – heads you get $10 million wired to your account, tails you receive nothing. The expected value of the coin toss is $5 million.

If you are like most people, you prefer the sure thing, the $5 million."

The participants that day had all selected the sure thing, although Jill had one person in her group who went for the coin toss. The facilitator had continued:

"The next step of the experiment is we keep the coin toss the same (heads you get $10 million, tails you get zero), but we reduce the sure thing to $4 million.

Now, which would you prefer?

You may be surprised to learn most people still prefer the sure thing, even when it's worth 20% less than the expected value of the coin toss."

Yup, all three members of Sellers' Club still preferred the sure thing. They remembered how everyone in training started both squirming in their seats and smiling as the discussion continued.

"According to classical economics" said the facilitator, "this is not rational behavior. Classical economists didn't factor in risk aversion – which is why it is a rational decision.

By now, you are probably thinking, where does the experiment stop? It continues till your breakeven point, the point at which you prefer the coin toss.

Maybe you are already there. We have had participants in our training say they wouldn't go for the coin toss until the sure thing was only $100,000.

The average break-even point is about $2.5 million sure thing, a 2:1 ratio of coin toss to sure thing.

This supports the old saying: 'A bird in the hand is worth two in the bush.'"

Everyone had enjoyed the coin toss experiment but wondered, 'what does this have to do with selling my business?' The facilitator continued:

"How does this apply to your buyer? Will the buyer see you as the sure thing or the coin toss?

Considered from the seller's perspective, you may see your business as the sure thing. Let's look at the buyer's perspective. Say the buyer is going to invest in a business. What alternative investments in a similar business does the buyer have, which will make your company seem like the coin toss?

What business would seem less risky than yours?"

Jim commented:

"This was probably the hardest part of the training, to fully grasp the buyer's sense of risk, to fully enter the buyer's mindset. Here are some answers we developed:

Perhaps another company has shown a stronger future team.

Or…

They have more recurring business and longer-term contracts.

Or…

The buyer already owns a company with a track record of requesting the investment amount you need and having paid back the money. Now, they are requesting a similar amount again.

Wouldn't the buyer feel more comfortable with the known quantity?"

Jill wanted to know: "How did this discussion lead you to hire a new key executive?"

Jim said: "I finally got the message about risk. In our first round of marketing, the bids were so-so. The marketing associates – who called the book holders – heard this too often: 'who is going to run the business in the future?'

That was the deciding factor for me. I had been considering hiring a strong potential replacement CEO for years. She had been in the industry for 20 years, was well-respected, and wanted to join my business. I hesitated because, well, what would I do if I hired her? Now, the situation is different; I want to exit.

In our next round of marketing, we featured the new hire in the one-page teaser. In the CIM, we said you will really want to meet our new CEO in a management meeting. What a difference this made in getting great LOIs with almost 100% cash at closing!" We have three strong management meetings coming up in the next week.

This Really Happened – Case Study

One of our clients reluctantly carved out two days for management meeting training – didn't think he would need it. At the outset, he was convinced:

- He would be the only participant in the management meetings
- His future team was solid

After the first day, he decided there was no future CEO on his team. The buyer would see risk. For years, this seller had been talking to a potential replacement CEO – an industry stalwart, with the exact successful leadership experience and temperament needed. The next morning, from 5:30 a.m. until 7:00 a.m., the seller was on the phone with his future CEO and they worked out a deal.

At lunch, on day two of training, he called his key execs, let them know he was looking for an investor, and invited their participation in the process. This took a great weight off his shoulders because:

- He really wanted to tell his key execs; they had been together so long and had such a great relationship.
- To get the virtual data room in shape by the due diligence deadline, he would need help from his key execs. So they would need to know what he was doing.

Are you ready to invite your key executives to the team?

Key Takeaways:

- Sellers typically don't see the risks that a buyer sees.

- Ask yourself this question: if I was buying my business, what risks would I see?

- Think about what you can do to be seen as the "sure thing."

- Buyers love to see recurring revenue and long term contracts

- Making sure you have a strong future team to deliver the future story reduces the buyer's sense of risk.

- If your CIM mentions the future team members who will attend management meetings, you will probably get more bids and higher bids.

Chapter 7

Is Your Business Sustainable? Beware of Self-Limiting Assumptions.

> What kind of crazy question is that? Of course my business is sustainable! By the way, what do you mean by sustainable?
> *The First-Time Seller's Question*
>
> I need to make sure the market is strong, the customers are loyal, and that we won't lose business when the seller retires.
> *The Buyer's Handbook*
>
> The buyer sees many unknowns we have to address. They don't know what we know.
> *The Seller's Handbook*

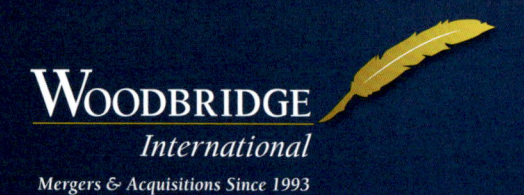

WOODBRIDGE *International*
Mergers & Acquisitions Since 1993

Sam was exasperated! He had been on the cusp of acquiring Jim's business – at a great price – five months ago. Now, he was part of the auction process, one of many bidders – which put the timeline out of his control – and the selling price kept increasing.

Sam's partners wanted to know if he was losing his touch. He wasn't losing his touch; it was this darn auction process! 'I would like to see any of my partners do better', he thought to himself.

On the other hand…

He attended the management meeting and was pleased to meet Jim's key execs and new CEO. Something he hadn't done the first time round.

Sam had begrudging respect for the auction process, though he wouldn't admit this to anyone. 'Maybe we should use this process when we sell our next business.'

More importantly he respected the improvements Jim implemented, coached by the M&A firm, which increased the business value. Sam actually picked up a few pointers which he could use when preparing his portfolio companies for sale.

Across town, Jim was meeting with the Sellers' Club to review where he was in the process and ask for their advice.

"I can see now why looking at the business sale from the buyer's perspective increases the perceived value to the buyer, particularly when addressing risk.

I thought it was a huge accomplishment to develop the strong future story – it created FOMO, fear of missing out, among many of the book holders. And it helped secure those strong non-binding bids.

I know we covered risk in management meeting training, but it wasn't real to me until qualified buyers in management meetings started asking the risk-related questions for which we had prepared."

Jill commented: "Bob and I completely understand; we went through the same journey into the buyer's mindset."

Jim wanted to talk. They listened:

"I was so focused on the future story – on creating FOMO, that I missed the power of risk mitigation in the auction process. Fortunately, I was committed to bringing in the future team, which helped make for powerful management meetings. In fact, publicizing we were bringing top execs brought two of the most qualified buyers to management meetings.

My first compelling evidence of the buyer's sense of risk came in the 'must-have questions' I received before the management meetings. Did you also get these?"

"Absolutely," agreed Bob and Jill.

"My closer secured these questions days in advance, which included:

- What percent of business is recurring? Under contract?
- What percent of business is contract based?
- What is the average duration of the 10 largest customers?

This caused a challenge at the outset."

Bob asked: "How so?"

"Half of our business is selling capital equipment. The customer doesn't return the following year to buy the equipment again."

Jill asked: "How did you handle this?"

"Our M&A firm showed us how to use two factors to reasonably forecast future sales from historical baseline data:

- Studying and confirming we have returning customers based on the 7-year life cycle of our equipment
- The add-on sales in the seven years after the purchase: We typically get 50 cents in add-on sales for every dollar spent in equipment in year one."

They all thought back to management meeting training, as the facilitator was explaining:

"Buyers want assurance your business is sustainable – that you have a strong flywheel concept – more on that in a moment; and that the market and your customer base will remain intact after you sell the business.

(Often, buyers fear you have inside information about imminent business decline and are looking to jump ship before the business crashes.)

Conceptually, we want to create both FOMO and a sense of low risk. You might ask, 'isn't it one or the other – either we have an exciting business, or we have a business which is very safe?'

72

This would be a 'Tyranny of OR' – a false alternative.

For the best auction, the best price and deal structure, we want to meet both essential buyer needs.

The risk assessment can be challenging to owners because, at the outset, we don't see any risk. We have been running the business for 10, 20, 30 or more years. Everything has been fine. It's in our bones. This is the seller's perspective.

The buyer lacks your granular long-standing tracking of the business. And your buyer has had bad experiences, where customers or key employees leave the business after the acquisition is made. So, they are cautious.

We need to beware a self-limiting assumption here – because we know the business is sustainable, the buyer will know this, sharing our perspective, without adequate proof."

Jill commented: "I loved the example of Roger Bannister overcoming the self-limiting assumption by running a four-minute mile in 1954. Until that time, it was thought to be impossible – human beings aren't designed to run a four-minute mile.

This helped me realize that I brought many self-limiting assumptions into this process."

Bob agreed: "Once I learned how to come down off the throne, I was open to learn and address many self-limiting assumptions, particularly as they relate to the buyer's perceived risks.

So, when the buyer asked, 'Will the customers and the business be there in the future'?, instead of getting annoyed, I offered proof. This led to strong LOIs from qualified buyers with certainty to close."

Jim added: "It was clear from the body language at the management meetings, we were connecting on risk issues.

Our presentation showed that both sides of our business – the equipment side and the services component – had these qualities:

- A fundamental, underlying, growing healthy market – that 'we are in the path of market growth'
- A predictable business – with long-tenured customers.

For the services component, the buyers loved seeing our long-term contracts with well-known customers. They also loved learning our sales department handles the relationships.

Better yet, they liked seeing a highly fragmented customer base so that no one customer has too large a share of our sales.

Jill added: "When I sold my business, I mitigated buyer risk by sharing a credible model for customer acquisition.

Many sellers are proud of the fact they 'do no advertising or selling. The customers come to us.'

This sounds great but leaves the buyer wondering: 'How can I ramp up sales and step on the gas'?

So, my prospective buyers were glad to hear:

- Our cost of customer acquisition is $1,125 per customer.
- We know this because we invest in pay per click, spending $5,000 per month.
- This generates 20 qualified leads a month, with a projected value of $200,000. We close about 20% of those leads, generating $40,000 in new business a month, getting an 8:1 payback on our investment of $5,000 a month. Closing four new clients a month, with a spend of $5,000, means a customer acquisition cost of $1,125."

In fact, one buyer commented:

'I appreciate the work you did documenting and proving out your model. Too many sellers don't do the analysis, making unproven claims like: 'It's easy to ramp up, just do some pay per click.' I can't pay them for this, which leads to conflict. You are making it easy to buy your business, Jill."

Bob added: "The same analysis can be made for expanding the sales team. Instead of saying 'go out and build or expand the sales team', we proved out the concept by hiring a salesperson, showing the buyer how easy it was to scale – and received credit for this in a higher selling price."

Jim thought he still had work to do on his flywheel concept:

"How was your flywheel presentation received?"

Jill was grateful for the coaching she received in designing her flywheel presentation, commenting:

"At first, I questioned how important it was to show a flywheel – the minimum set of business qualities which lead to a predictable recurring business. With our M&A company's help, we designed this flywheel statement:

- High repeat annual business – over 90% recurring from existing customers
- Proprietary software
- Strong, long-term relationships with OEMs and other vendor partners
- Wide range of services from network planning, testing, optimization and installation as well as compliance and staffing services
- Scalability
- Offshore resources

Jim was going to work on his flywheel for the next management meeting.

This Really Happened – Case Histories

In developing your minimum sell price, the theme of fair and reasonable is essential. For example, we had one client who wasn't fair and reasonable. A project-based company, doing about $1 million in EBITDA, had one fantastic month. They actually earned

$1 million from a non-recurring project. The client wanted a new annual EBITDA calculation, of $12 million EBITDA, to get paid on that basis. But they couldn't show the income would be recurring. The client dug in, and the business became unsellable.

We had a client who sold into the jet engine market, where there are essentially three customers: Rolls Royce, GE and Pratt & Whitney. There's an automatic concentration/risk issue. Since most of their sales were with one of the three, there was 90% customer concentration.

With some creative analysis, we lowered the buyer's blood pressure and sense of risk. The seller made over 1,500 different parts for their major client. This showed that the overall relationship wasn't at risk – the 1,500 individual parts were at risk. They would lose some of these from time to time; but often, the customer would return to them, because only they could deliver the quality needed for the precision parts. Properly presented, the buyer understood there was substantial diversification.

A client's service business was strongly impacted by recent supply line issues. We were able to secure an $11 million offer for this company with $2.5 million in EBITDA. However, because of the supply line issues, the owner only received $6.5 million at close, the balance in earnout. The buyer saw risk.

Buyers will not only want to know you have recurring business, but also: What is the quality of your business relationships?

At the end of their due diligence analysis, most buyers will want to make discrete phone calls to major customers, to test your relationships. Are these relationships solid, are they too dependent on the owners?

We recently sold a technology company where the three owners controlled all the major relationships. With $4 million in EBITDA, it was valued at $29.5 million; however, the buyer required the sellers to take 35% rollover equity, with only $18 million cash at closing. Why? The buyer wanted the sellers to have a stake in maintaining the essential relationships into the future.

The book *E Myth* resonates here – buyers prefer owners who work "on the business" to owners who work "in the business."

E Myth compares the McDonald brothers who liked making hamburgers to Ray Kroc who built the McDonald franchise system. The McDonald brothers worked in the business, making hamburgers. Ray Kroc worked on the business, developing the franchise system.

When an owner works "on the business," when they aren't intimately involved in all the operations, the buyer feels more comfortable with the owner leaving the business. The buyer can pay more money, more cash at closing.

We saw the *E Myth* difference with a distributor client, who had almost $3.5 million in EBITDA. He received $18.5 million in cash at closing, in part because the owner wasn't visibly associated with the business – it ran without him. His name wasn't on the website, he didn't talk to any customers. The buyer felt comfortable paying more cash at closing.

How can we address the buyers' relationship concerns earlier in the process to get more bids and then more LOIs?

Do you have strong testimonial – letters or even better – do you have video testimonials? For an example of powerful video testimonials, take a look at our website: https://woodbridgegrp.com/testimonials.

Something else you might share, where appropriate, are scorecards – evaluations you have received from major Fortune 500 companies. (You may have to conceal the source, because of confidentiality agreements.)

Is your business sustainable in the eyes of the buyer?

Key Takeaways:

- *The buyer wants to make sure your business is sustainable – has a strong enough underlying market and that you have a strong business model.*

- *What is your flywheel? The basic elements that lead to replicable business year in and year out.*

- *Buyers are more comfortable when you have a greater percent of your business under long-term contract or with recurring revenue from long-tenured customers.*

- *Buyers like to see trusted advisor relationships.*

- *The more you can show the buyer you are working on the business vs. in the business, the less risk the buyer will see.*

- *Bring your customer testimonials and scorecards to the discussion.*

WOODBRIDGE
International

1764 Litchfield Turnpike | Suite 250 | New Haven, CT 06525
203.389.8400 | woodbridgegrp.com

" Of course my business is defendable. I micromanage every aspect of it, keeping a sharp eye on and one step ahead of my competition.

The First-Time Seller's Question

Is the business strategy defendable without the owner?

The Buyer's Handbook

The more we show uncontested space, the more comfortable the buyer will be.

The Seller's Handbook "

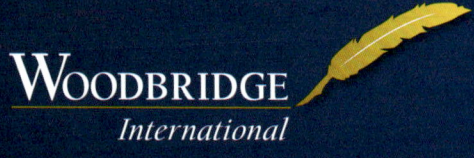

WOODBRIDGE
International
Mergers & Acquisitions Since 1993

Sam was still in the running to buy Jim's business; only he wasn't sure he should be glad of this. A week had gone by, and the M&A firm had called for final offers to be delivered today. It seemed like there were at least two other motivated buyers. Who wanted to be in a bidding war? The investment committee had already given him authority to increase his offer to 40% over the initial offer. But should he?

Of course, with the new CIM and management meeting presentation, the business was clearly worth more; Jim was now showing a strong future story and management team and overall lower perceived risk.

Sam turned his thoughts to defendability. Would competitors enter and take away significant business after the sale?

He thought about business school and the case method. Business history is replete with cases of first-to-market innovators with a sustainable product they couldn't defend.

Consider the soda innovator RC Cola…

At the same time, Jim was teeing up a cup of Joe at Sellers' Club. It was a week after their last meeting. Today was the day.

Last best offers were due from three qualified and motivated buyers at 4 p.m., including one from Sam – his original buyer. What a difference the auction process could make!

Jim wanted to revisit his defensive position with Jill and Bob. He was thinking about RC Cola and what he learned in management meeting training. He heard the facilitator's voice in his mind:

"Do you know what RC Cola innovated in 1958?

They brought out the first diet cola.

Was it sustainable, is there diet cola demand to this day? Absolutely!

Was it defendable? No. Today, most people would ask for a Diet Coke or Diet Pepsi. Diet Coke and Diet Pepsi dominate the market.

Buyers know about these cases, have typically been on the losing end of an undefendable market at some point, and want to ensure your position is defendable.

Earlier, we talked about a client who sold one product to one customer. They were a concentration risk. However, as the world's low-cost producer, very defendable.

In the 2004 book Blue Ocean Strategy, the authors encourage us to look for blue oceans of uncontested space. Too many companies live in "red oceans" of cutthroat competition.

The low-cost producer we discussed occupied uncontested space.

Buyers love to hear we have uncontested space."

Jim emerged from his reverie.

Bob commented: "You look very thoughtful today, Jim. What's on your mind, besides coffee."

Jim responded: "Last best offers are due today from three committed, qualified buyers. I was thinking about the journey

I made in the last five months. At the outset, I was only talking to Sam's firm, who offered:

$8.5 million, 60% cash at closing, with the balance in a note over three years – after the buyer completes due diligence, no set closing date.

Here is where the process has brought me today:

- Sam's firm: $10.5 million, 85% cash at closing, balance in one year, 60 days to close
- Buyer B: $11 million, 10% in equity rollover, $2 million in a 3-year note; 60 days to close
- Buyer C: $10 million, all cash at closing, 75 days to close

Jill was curious: "Are you leaning in one direction or another, assuming the final bids are ranked the same way?"

Jim continued to be thoughtful: "At the outset of the auction process, I was angry at Sam, and didn't want to do business with his firm. I liked him, I liked our cultural fit, but thought he took advantage of me, when I was uneducated.

As we got deeper into the process, I realized I didn't initially give Sam a strong enough case to offer a better deal. It wasn't his fault, it was mine.

So, I really wouldn't mind if he was the auction finalist.

But what's mostly on my mind is: Did I do a good enough job in de-risking my business? Did I show the buyers there is a strong defensive position?

If you don't mind, I would like to do a checklist review with you, for both uncontested space and barriers to entry:

- Long-term contracts cover 10% of our service sales
- Recurring service revenue for 70% of our service sales, which are 50% of our sales; with average customer duration of 10 years
- Exclusive distribution agreements cover 30% of our equipment sales
- Intellectual property – patents, trademarks – cover another 20% of our equipment sales
- Trusted advisor relationships with all key customers, with the relationships managed by the sales team
- High switching costs cover another 20% of our sales

Overall, I would say 70% of total sales are defended by uncontested space or high switching costs.

Can you think of any holes in our strategic story?

Jill wanted to know: "On a level playing field, if you go up against your top 3-4 competitors, how often do you win?"

Jim was proud to say: "About 70% of the time."

"That's great," said Jill.

Bob had another question: "What if I decided to start a greenfield operation? What would it cost? How long would it take me to get to your current market share?"

Jim wasn't sure. His best guess was: $5 million to start from scratch, then a minimum of 5-10 years to build the EBITDA, assuming you could take away my customers. We would try to prevent that."

Both Jill and Bob thought Jim had a strong defensive case.

This Really Happened – Case Histories

- **Too dependent on the seller**

    The seller had built a wonderful service business. The owner had developed two important networks: unique, skilled service providers around the world and Fortune 500 companies who sponsored events where the unique service was the main draw.

    By meeting these needs, the owner earned about $3 million in EBITDA; we were able to find a buyer paying $16 million. The problem was the deal structure. The buyer was concerned the seller – who only wanted to remain one year – was essential to maintaining and building the Fortune 500 customer relationships.

    To protect against the seller leaving too early, the buyer offered this deal structure: 25% cash at closing; then 25% for each of the next three years.

    You wouldn't want to wait three years for your money. Neither did the seller. We found another buyer, who would pay 50% cash at closing, acceptable to the seller.

- **Too dependent on the seller, concern about key employees leaving**

    In a recent case, still not resolved, the seller had started his service business when his last employer didn't want to take on a contract from a national company. Our client – learning about the opportunity – grabbed three skilled technicians and started the business. So far, in management meetings, buyers expressed concern the same thing could happen again – skilled technicians might leave the company and start a new company. The owner – in his late 60's and wanting to retire – made the situation even worse, by boasting how important he was to all the relationships.

- **Exclusive distribution agreements, well established brand**

    Our client was the exclusive North American distributor for a high-end, branded backyard accessory, imported from Europe. With $2.5 MM in EBITDA, and an established customer and dealer network, our client was paid $11 million, mostly cash at closing.

    However, the distributor agreement was based on a handshake. The European factory knew and trusted our client for over 10 years. The seller didn't see any risk.

    How would a buyer feel about paying $11 million for a company which depended on a handshake agreement with their source of supply? Would you buy this company?

Before we went to market, we coached the client to secure a written agreement. This was just table stakes for engaging prospective buyers.

Ultimately, the buyer made some modifications to the distribution agreement; fortunately, all three parties – the buyer, seller, and European manufacturer – were committed to the deal and it got done.

With the new agreement in place, the buyers felt comfortable with uncontested space, locking up a great brand.

This story also illustrates the importance of using your M&A resource as a sounding board when accepting an LOI (letter of intent).

- **High switching costs**

    A client provided IT support to Fortune 500 customers around the world. Once their technicians were in place, because of the project length and the long learning curve, there were very high switching costs. This is a major reason the buyer was willing to pay $27 million for the company's $4 million in EBITDA. They had a strong defensive position.

    A similar scenario involved a title company handling real estate closings. Once they became part of the bank's closing "team," they did such a good job, the relationship was very sticky. We were able to get the owner $21 million, about 7x EBITDA, with $18 million cash at closing.

- **Trusted advisor relationships (with high switching costs)**

    A client had worked with all major utilities in a Western state for over 40 years. They knew where practically 'every foot of cable was located underground'; they had deep relationships with the clients. Supply line disruptions halted installations in the recent year, with EBITDA falling to $270,000. With a $70 million backlog in business and their close relationships with the utilities, the buyer was willing to pay our client $15 million, based on the last strong year of sales.

- **Dilemmas**

    A dilemma is a self-inflicted wound by a competitor. Who should have won the PC wars, Apple or IBM? Why didn't IBM win? IBM saw computing as centralized and was never fully committed to the PC product.

    One of our clients offered customized installations of product lines available at Home Depot. As long as Home Depot is committed to "do it yourself," they probably won't enter the client's space.

    If you can show your major competition avoids your market space, this is a big plus.

Can you show that your major competition avoids your market space? This is a big plus.

Key Takeaways:

- Buyers like to see uncontested markets, with high barriers to entry. What gives your business these qualities?

- Can you show the buyer any of these defendable positions?
    - Low-cost producer
    - High switching costs
    - Brands
    - Intellectual property

- If we don't show a defendable position, or if you are too important to the business, don't be surprised if buyers want to pay through an earnout over time.

WOODBRIDGE *International*

1764 Litchfield Turnpike | Suite 250 | New Haven, CT 06525
203.389.8400 | woodbridgegrp.com

Chapter 9

Selecting Your Deal Attorney – Someone Who Understands Deals

> That's an easy call; I'll use my contracts attorney; we've worked together for 20 years.
> — **The First-Time Seller's Question**
>
> Hopefully, the seller will disclose everything to maintain trust and will select a strong, knowledgeable deal attorney who can get the deal done.
> — **The Buyer's Handbook**
>
> Disclose for trust and select an attorney who understands that time kills all deals.
> — **The Seller's Handbook**

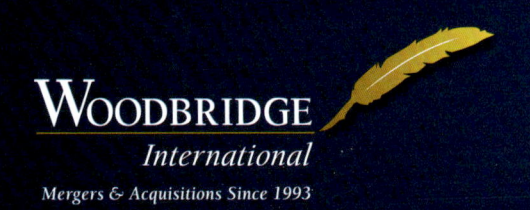

WOODBRIDGE *International*
Mergers & Acquisitions Since 1993

"I wonder," thought Jim. "Should I tell them about that bogus lawsuit? The trumped-up case by my disgruntled ex-employee who claimed I fired him for no good reason?"

That was two months ago. The M&A firm had recommended: 'disclose'. In fact, they advised 'disclose it in the CIM. Buyers don't like discovering an undisclosed lawsuit in due diligence. They begin to wonder what else you didn't disclose. Buyers need to see transparency and feel trust if a deal is going to close on time.'

In retrospect, it was good advice. The frivolous lawsuit was disclosed in the CIM; doing so hadn't prevented a robust auction with over 25 bids. It seemed like an embarrassment of riches. Jim wondered: 'Who should I invite to management meetings?'

This was one of two major reasons Jim was at Sellers' Club today – to ask Bob and Jill who he should invite to the management meeting. The other reason was to get advice on selecting a deal lawyer.

"I wonder," thought Jim. "Who should I select as my deal lawyer?" His first impulse was to select his business attorney, having relied on her for over 20 years, to help with contracts, labor issues, etc. "Why shouldn't I call on her to handle the business sale?"

Still, Jim wasn't sure. This seemed a good subject to discuss at Sellers' Club. Today, Jim was the early bird, and was waiting with a cup of Joe, as Bob and Jill joined him.

Jill asked how the business sale was going. They hadn't seen Jim in two weeks.

"I am very pleased overall. We have over 15 bids."

"I held back on selecting a lawyer and now I'm stuck. It's time to decide. I have worked with my business lawyer, Donna, for over 20 years. I asked her if she does deals, she said 'yes'. She is totally trustworthy, in fact, a trusted advisor. She has a good grasp of both my business and the legal documents that go with my business.

The M&A firm introduced me to their recommended deal lawyer. He seems OK, but I've known Donna for over 20 years. How do I make a good decision?"

Jill wanted to know: "What is most important to you – that you use a lawyer that you know or that you get a great outcome?"

Jim smiled: "When you put it that way it's obvious – I want a great outcome. The question is: 'Why can't Donna get me a great outcome?'"

Bob said: "Maybe she can. Did you peel back the onion? How many deals did she do in the last year? How many on the buyer's side, how many on the seller's side?"

Jim admitted: "I never asked her that question, but why is it relevant?"

Jill chimed in: "How do you satisfy yourself that Donna knows 'what is market?' If you get pushed around by a Wall Street law firm that says, 'I've been doing deals this way for 30 years', can she defend you? Can she tell you what is fair and reasonable?"

Jim said: "She will want to defend me; I'm not sure yet that she can."

Bob commented: "Here are some other things to consider – does she have the bandwidth to stick to the timeline? You know that time kills all deals; will she be able to keep up with a 60-day due diligence/closing schedule? The reasonable buyer wants you to select an attorney who knows how to do deals.

And how about this one – can she evaluate if the buyer's lawyer is going to be reasonable? With all the bids you received, one of your screening criteria could be: does the buyer have a reasonable lawyer. Can Donna assess that?"

Jim looked glum: "I'm beginning to think maybe she's not the right deal lawyer. But I don't know how I can face her and tell her she's not doing the deal after she told me she does deals."

Jill pointed out: "You can still keep her involved in the deal. Maybe she can oversee getting all the contracts and documentation you will need."

Jim brightened up at this thought. He felt Donna helped bring him to the dance, and he didn't want to exclude her.

This left Jim with one major question: 'Who should I invite to management meetings?'

He put the question on the table: "Here is a recap of my bids; who would you invite?"

To see the bid spreadsheet, cllck
https://woodbridgegrp.com/bidspreadsheets.

Bob said: "I think the best advice we can give you is asking: Who gives you the most of what you want?"

Jim said: "Well, first of all, certainty to close. When I consider only the well-funded bidders, we are down to 10."

94

Jill asked: "What else matters to you?"

Jim responded: "Well, I don't want to be part of the transition for more than one year. I want a buyer who will take care of my employees and has a track record of holding investments. And I need a minimum of $X at closing."

Bob wanted to know: "How many contenders are left?"

Jim said: "Looks like just four or five; that makes my life easy."

Take a look at this URL and try to determine who you would bring to the management meeting.

This is an actual bid spread sheet provided to a client with names removed. Click https://woodbridgegrp.com/bidspreadsheets.

This Really Happened – Case History

Here's a case of a deal lawyer who understood deals, but worked at his own pace:

We had a drop-dead closing date of March 15th. Our client selected a lawyer who understood transactions but moved at his own pace. So we missed the drop-dead closing date.

Then, a black swan event occurred. The seller leased one of their two facilities. Their lease agreement had the following clause – the landlord had to give two years notice if they were going to sell the building. The seller received notice, after March 15th.

Fortunately, the buyer was committed. They still bought the

business. But there had to be an allowance made for moving the business in two years.

So, of the $8 million selling price, $1 million was put in escrow to pay for moving the business in two years. If we had closed on the drop-dead closing date, if we had a lawyer who honored the timeline, it wouldn't have been our problem.

Time continues to kill all deals.

At Woodbridge, we will advise you on lawyers who can work to our timeline.

 Everything will come out in due diligence. When the buyer is alerted to an issue in due diligence, the thought process is: "What else didn't they tell me?"

One of our favorite legal resources teaches us: "It's better to be a footnote in the CIM (confidential information memo) than a special addendum during due diligence."

What does this mean?

When we disclose something in the CIM, it's 'priced into the deal.' When it comes out in due diligence, it destroys trust. "Why didn't you tell us this," thinks the buyer. "What else didn't you tell us?"

This analysis suggests you should have some legal counsel early in the selling process to determine what needs to be disclosed.

 One client – providing counseling services – didn't disclose a tragedy had occurred on their watch: a client had committed suicide, resulting in a lawsuit. This came out in due diligence.

Fortunately, the buyer was motivated and bought the company, albeit with price adjustments. However, the seller needlessly undermined trust. A strong deal lawyer, as well as your M&A company, will provide needed guidance here.

There is a "pay me now or pay me later" aspect to when you engage your deal attorney. If you bring them in early, you have bills earlier. If you bring them in later, you may have a ticking time bomb in your CIM.

It's pay me now or pay me later, but we always pay. How do you want to pay?

Key Takeaways:

- Your deal lawyer selection is often a "make or break" decision – critical to the deal's success.

- Involve your lawyer early enough in the transaction to make sure you present the right offer to the marketplace.

- Select a lawyer who has enough transaction experience to know what is market and what is not reasonable.

- Beware of selecting your contracts lawyer if he or she doesn't have much deal experience.

- Be a success story, not a statistic. There are few real deal killers, if you have a strong legal advisor.

WOODBRIDGE
International

1764 Litchfield Turnpike | Suite 250 | New Haven, CT 06525
203.389.8400 | woodbridgegrp.com

Chapter 10
Summing Up:
The Buyer's Perspective

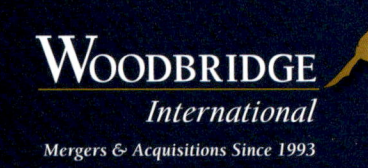

Sam felt a sense of deja vu. A few short months ago, he was expecting to sign an LOI with Jim at noon. Well, today at noon, he would hear Jim's final decision. Would Jim sign his LOI or that of another buyer? Sam felt out of control.

Jim also felt a sense of deja vu. He remembered going to Sellers' Club the first time, when he was about to sign an LOI with Sam.

Well, Sam was still in the running, one of three, and the LOIs were a lot sweeter than Sam's original offer.

Jill and Bob welcomed him. Bob asked: "What's on your mind today?"

"It's decision time, which LOI will I sign."

He brought a recap sheet to the meeting. *(Please see next page.)*

Jim continued by thanking Bob and Jill: "Without your advice, I never would have had an auction, which produced deals substantially better than the one I had the day we first met."

Bob said: "Glad to hear it. Just curious, what were your biggest takeaways from our meetings?"

Jim rattled off a few things:

"Mostly about mindset, for example:

- **Pay me now or pay me later –**
  There is no cheating reality. It's usually better to pay now. For example, bringing my exec team to the management meeting. Even Sam claimed this made a difference, got him to increase his offer.

- **Overcoming self-limiting assumptions –**
  Addressing risk.

- **Tyranny of the OR –**
  Instead of: Do you want me to maintain EBITDA or populate the data room? I learned I needed to do both; I needed an AND."

- **The burden-of-proof criteria –**
  It's up to me to prove the assertions I make, particularly about the future story and seeing the buyer's sense of risk, where I see none.

Letter of Intent (LOI) Recap Sheet

Terms *(Dollars in Millions)*	Buyer 1
Purchase Price (EV) - $ in Millions	$11.0
Real Estate	Lease
Cash at Close	$7.26
Seller Note	-
Seller Note Period	-
Equity Roll	$0.438
Earnout	$3.30
Earnout Period	18 Months
Common Equity	-
Escrow	$1.00
Escrow period	18 Months
Net Working Capital	king capital as compared to a normalized
Due Diligence/Timing	90 Days

Number of Acquisitions	3
Operation Partner	Need to recruit
Contract with Vendors	5 Year extension
WB History/Relationship:	2 Completed Deals
Employment contract for seller	Extend Employment Agreement, 1 Year Period, $150,000.00 annual salary, including performance based bonus incentives, Preferred he takes position as Board of Directors

Maybe most importantly:

- **Coming down off the throne – and being humble."**

Jill smiled and said: "Not a bad ROI, for the price of a cup of coffee."

Bob said: "That still leaves open one question, which LOI are you going to sign?"

I think Jim needs your help. Which LOI would you sign?

Buyer 2	Buyer 3
$11.0	$10.9
Lease	$0.40
$8.14	$8.65
-	$1.25
-	6 Year Note, 5% Annual IR, 15 year ammortization
$0.658	-
$2.20	-
18 Months	-
-	$0.99
$0.88	-
12 Months	-
ing capital as compared to a normalized	Yes, Value Adjustment at close based on NWC
60 Days	70-75 Days

3	35
Need to recruit	Jeff
-	-
2 Completed Deals	1 Completed Deal
Extend Employment Agreement, 1 Year Period, $150,000.00 annual salary, including performance based bonus incentives, Preferred he takes position as Board of Directors	SCC is accustomed to seller transitions of 3-6 months; however, the buyer would like the timing for this transition to be flexible, and the Buyer will work with the Seller to develop a plan that makes sense for all parties

About the Author
Professor Gole

Andy Gole has been a member of team Woodbridge since November 2016.

He has been the facilitator of Woodbridge's 2-day Management Meeting Training. As of March, 2022 he has held 64 training sessions.

Prior to joining Woodbridge, Andy was an adjunct professor for 8 years at the Rothman Institute for Entrepreneurial Studies at FDU in NJ – teaching small business management. He has been a consultant to over 120 companies and is the author of the book, Innovate Now. He holds an MBA in Marketing from NYU.